EUREKA!

POEMS ABOUT INVENTORS

EUREKA!

Poems About Inventors

JOYCE SIDMAN

809.1
Sid   Sidman, Joyce.
    Eureka! : poems about
    inventors

00201227

Illustrated by K. Bennett Chavez

THE MILLBROOK PRESS   BROOKFIELD, CONNECTICUT

*To my parents, Robert and Elizabeth, who always steered
me toward excellence.*

—J. S.

To my husband Raul.

—K. B. C.

About the title of this book

The expression "Eureka!" originates in a legend told about Archimedes (c. 287–212 B.C.),
a brilliant Greek mathematician known as the father of experimental science. Charged
with determining the amount of gold in the king's crown, he noticed one day while
bathing that the deeper he sank into the tub, the more water spilled from it. Realizing he
had found the key to measuring the volume of an irregular solid, he leaped from the bath
and ran toward the palace naked, crying, "Eureka!" (meaning "I found it!" in Greek).

Published by The Millbrook Press, Inc.
2 Old New Milford Road
Brookfield, CT 06804

Text copyright © 2002 by Joyce Sidman
Illustrations copyright © 2002 by K. Bennett Chavez
All rights reserved

Library of Congress Cataloging-in-Publication Data
Sidman, Joyce.
Eureka! : poems about inventors / Joyce Sidman ; illustrated by Kristen Chavez.
p. cm.
ISBN 0-7613-1665-5 (lib. bdg.)
1. Inventors—Juvenile poetry. 2. Children's poetry, American. [1. Inventors—Poetry.
2. American poetry.] I. Chavez, Kristen, ill. II. Title.
PS3569.I295 W5 2001   811'.54—dc21   00-056620

"An Evening Among Peach Blossoms" and "A Length of Pink Ribbon" previously appeared in
Cicada magazine

Printed in the United States of America
1 3 5 4 2

"Necessity is the Mother of Invention."
—Anonymous

"Creativity is the sudden cessation of stupidity."
—Edwin Land

"Who never walks save where he sees men's tracks makes no discoveries."
—J.G. Holland

CONTENTS

The Tapestry of the Past

The Age of Invention

A Light Interlude

Dawn of the Modern Age

THE
TAPESTRY
OF
THE PAST

PREHISTORY
(*The discovery of clay*)

By the river,
she finds a bush of early berries
and picks hungrily
as the children shriek and wallow
in the heavy orange mud.
The sun is hot as furred skin,
the water cool, with a promise of meat.
Her man wades downriver,
hoping the silvertails
will swim into his waiting hand.

So many berries!

She cannot hold all their
tumbling sweetness.
Moans her frustration—
weeks of so little,
and now so much!
And no way to carry it.
Flies weave dizzy clouds
around her red-stained face.
Impatiently she turns
to where the children lie, drowsing
in the sun. The strange orange mud
has dried on their legs.
She peels off a tough crust
and taps it. Hard as wood.
Rounded from the calf of her child.

A vessel, to carry berries.

A bowl.

Suddenly she dives, breathless,
toward the river and its mud,
to seize the bright, dripping shape
of an idea.

An Evening Among Peach Blossoms

*(Ts'ai Lun developed the method of making true
paper in A.D. 105.)*

Dawn comes silently
like a lover's embrace.
My Lady Who Writes,
in a few short hours I will present you
with your heart's desire.
But in this soft light
I think of the past,
when we bent our heads together.

I can still see you,
new to the court as I was,
slim and plain as a nightingale.
You turned away jewels and bright robes
for scrolls and ink.
You were a great scholar, even then.
The words you painted on silk
glimmered like the dawning sun
that rises, in time,
to its true power.

I, for my cleverness,
caught your eye.
"Ts'ai Lun!" you called
in your bird's voice.
"I must write, yet silk is costly.

There is never enough.
Find me something I can write upon!"

Sixteen years I labored,
searching the countryside,
mixing and scraping and stretching
anything I could find.
I lived for the moment
I could bring my humble offerings
to your sight, watch your white hand
move over the page.
"No," you would say softly,
"it is not good enough, Ts'ai Lun.
Keep working."
And I would bow, joyful
that the task was still before me.

The sun, which rises now
above the garden, dries and cures my work.
Smooth and perfect,
the paper awaits your brush.
Soon I will see your hand
fly like the white breast of a swallow
across the page.
Sixteen years was like an evening
spent among peach blossoms.
I, clever Ts'ai Lun,
half-a-man,
lament that my task is done.

WINGED WORDS

*(Johann Gutenberg was the inventor of
mechanical printing and movable type.)*

In a small, dark shop in Mainz
Johann Gutenberg toils
to the voice of the Rhine
outside his window,
that black growl of water
fraying the ancient battlements.
Like a man asleep, he cuts and polishes
gemstones for the rich,
mirrors for the not-so-rich,
cheap jewelry for those like himself
who have little to spare for trinkets.

But he dreams—oh! he dreams
of glittering piles of letters:
metal-cast letters that sit heavily in the hand
and slide together with a sweet click,
making words.
He dreams of inking and wiping them,
pressing them to thick, creamy vellum.

Money, when he gets it,
fuels only the forge of his desire.
Years blend together
as ever again, the dream begins:
pouring lead into hand-carved molds,
tumbling out the red-hot letters.
Hour after hour
sliding letters into words,
grouping words into sentences.
Sheets peel off the presses of his mind:
psalms, verses, texts—the Lord's book!

The Rhine grinds its stones
with the cool, dark voice of ruin.
Gutenberg hears only
the flocks and flocks of
lovely Latin script,
flying like God's doves
into the future.

"In the beginning was the word ..."

WIZARD

(Leonardo da Vinci—artist, engineer, cartographer,
and scientist—lived from 1452 to 1519.)

They think I am a wizard,
think their petty wars demonstrate
what power there is on earth.
"Leonardo," they say, "build me a rampart
that can never be scaled, to foil the Venetians."
"Leonardo, with this statue we must impress the Duke."
"Design a grand pageant for the court, Leonardo!"
I fashion deadly toys
to defend their precious bits of stone
and while they strut like warring cocks
I slip away to the green hills above the Arno.

These are the things I think about:
   Do men have enough muscles to fly?
   Might not the same power that moves one gear move twenty?
   Does every flower demonstrate the principles of geometry?
   Where in the body does the soul reside?
I lean against the ancient shoulders of the earth and wonder:
   How long does it take water to erode a mountain?
   Can one divert a river?
   Why do objects in the distance appear smaller?
   Is beauty given for a purpose?

I am like the one who arrives last at the fair
after the hawking and the hoopla and the heavy press of flesh
to find only trinkets, bits of ribbons,
a bundle of reeds, a bird feather.
With a sly grin I pocket these things of little value,
knowing I can create from them wonders
such as the world has never seen.

We know little about how humans lived before recorded history. Inventions that made life easier probably arose either of necessity or in brief moments of safety when the mind was free. We do know this: No single person invented such ordinary objects as the chair, hat, wheel, or whistle. In pockets of primitive culture throughout the inhabited world, these basic inventions were developed, forgotten, redeveloped, and refined until gradually they gained universal usage.

Ts'ai Lun was a eunuch in Emperor Ho-ti's court in the Hunan Province of China. Known for his cleverness, he was commissioned by Queen Dun-Shi, a noted scholar, to find a cheaper and more abundant writing material than silk. In A.D. 105, after sixteen years of scouring the countryside for materials, he finally settled on a mixture of mulberry bark and hemp. Soaking and stirring the fibers until they fell apart, he spread the pulp over a mesh-covered bamboo frame and dried it in the sun. The result was a sheet of true paper. Some say Ts'ai Lun discovered this method after watching wasps chewing wood to make their papery nests.

Johann Gutenberg was born in Mainz in 1399, at a time when few people knew how to read. Books were hand copied by monks or scribes and used only by the Church and the privileged classes. Gutenberg, whose parents were landed gentry of modest means, began experimenting with movable-type letters that could be rearranged to print different words. Unlike others before him, he used metal, which was longer lasting, instead of wood or porcelain. In 1454, after decades of false starts, he published two hundred copies of the world's first printed text. This extraordinarily beautiful edition of the Bible is still treasured today by those few museums fortunate enough to own one of the original copies.

Leonardo da Vinci is best known for his painted masterpiece, the *Mona Lisa*, but he had many other talents. In his notebooks he described ideas for inventions, precisely sketched the natural world, and recorded scientific experiments, often in mirror writing, or backward script. Some of his inventions—steam cannon, helicopter, and bicycle—were so brilliantly ahead of his time that they were not developed for centuries. For wealthy patrons, he created weapons, fortifications, and elaborate stage events. But the power he respected the most was nature: its life-threatening force, breathtaking beauty, and endless diversity.

THE AGE
OF
INVENTION

THOSE FABULOUS FRENCHMEN
(The Montgolfier brothers invented the hot-air balloon.)

They played around a lot with fire,
Joe and Jacques Montgolfier—
set the harvest grass alight
and watched the blue smoke whirl away.

One of them—we're not sure which—
to feed the dying embers, chose
to burn an empty paper bag.
It filled with blackened air and rose!

They tried again, experimented,
and, perfecting their balloon,
they launched a duck into the air
above Versailles one afternoon.

It worked! And shortly after that,
Jacques Charles, another Frenchman, found
a lovely gas called hydrogen
would take him farther off the ground.

Then there was Jean-Pierre Blanchard,
who, not content to merely float
across the English Channel, used
two silken oars to steer his "boat"!

He made it, by some miracle,
and gay Paree went balloon-mad.
Many flew and many crashed
amid this aeronautic fad.

Balloons? They've gone the way of horses:
cumbersome and rather rare,
but they were first to lift us up
into the bright, enchanted air.

FOOD OF THE GODS
(François-Louis Cailler created the first chocolate bar in 1819.)

In the time before memory,
Quetzalcoatl—the Plumed Serpent—
dropped ripe yellow pods of cacao
into the steamy jungle,
a gift to lowly man.
He taught the Aztec how to grow
its broad-leaved trees,
how to split the pod's soft pulp
for the almond-shaped beans,
how to roast them and pound them to dust
and make of them *tchocolatl*:
the thick bitter drink of the gods.
Then He set sail for the land
where the sun rests at night,
promising one day to come back.

When Cortéz marched up the Aztec highway
and appeared, pale-skinned,
like the god returning,
it was *tchocolatl* Montezuma offered him
in a goblet of gold.
Offered, too, his life's blood,
his heart, his kingdom.

Bound in fragrant sacks,
the beans crossed oceans, rivers, Alps,
where Cailler seized upon them,
mixed and ground and tempered,
and by some clean and wholesome magic,
made of them a food—
a wafer of heaven,
a smooth slab of heart's delight.

As the first crumbs melted in his mouth,
could he taste that faint bitterness,
that single dark tear
from the eye of
the ancient god?

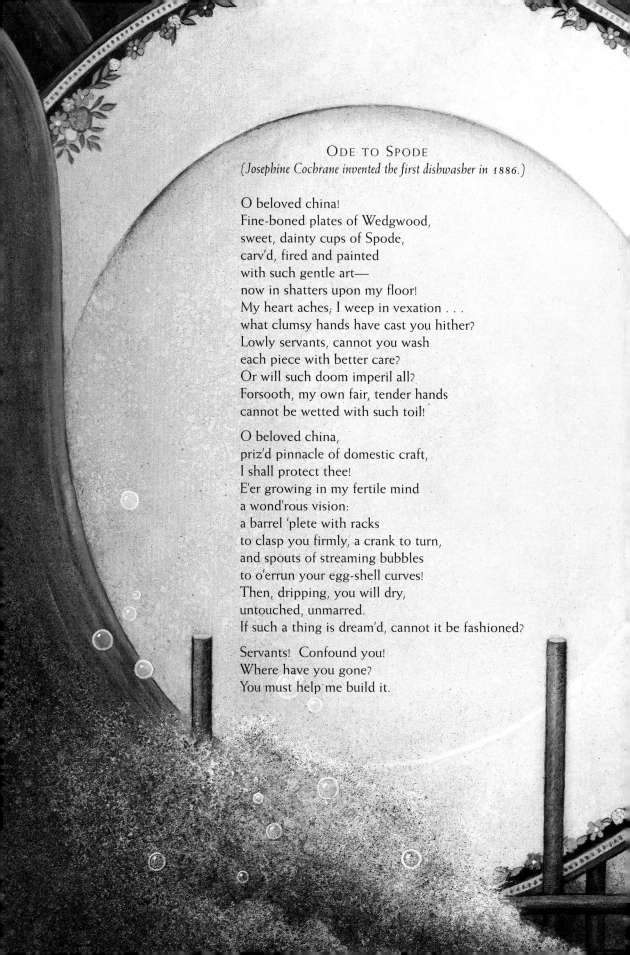

ODE TO SPODE

(Josephine Cochrane invented the first dishwasher in 1886.)

O beloved china!
Fine-boned plates of Wedgwood,
sweet, dainty cups of Spode,
carv'd, fired and painted
with such gentle art—
now in shatters upon my floor!
My heart aches; I weep in vexation . . .
what clumsy hands have cast you hither?
Lowly servants, cannot you wash
each piece with better care?
Or will such doom imperil all?
Forsooth, my own fair, tender hands
cannot be wetted with such toil!

O beloved china,
priz'd pinnacle of domestic craft,
I shall protect thee!
E'er growing in my fertile mind
a wond'rous vision:
a barrel 'plete with racks
to clasp you firmly, a crank to turn,
and spouts of streaming bubbles
to o'errun your egg-shell curves!
Then, dripping, you will dry,
untouched, unmarred.
If such a thing is dream'd, cannot it be fashioned?

Servants! Confound you!
Where have you gone?
You must help me build it.

THERE IS A CRAVING
(Dr. Sara J. Baker invented a safe method for dispensing silver nitrate, to prevent blindness at birth.)

There is a craving
deep inside
that starts when you first realize
you've got the frosting on the cake
when others don't even have
the flour to make it.
A craving to even up that score,
to work with a strong back
and a clear eye that takes in
the worst that life can offer.

Sometimes, though,
when I'm tired and the world's grime
seems to rise up in a wave
over all that is good and beautiful,
I wish I hadn't seen that raggedy girl
on the morning of my sixth birthday,
hadn't taken the measure of her calico
against my velvet
and decided where the need lay.
Every stitch I gave her, hairbow to socks.
Mother didn't say a word.

Yet even in Hell's Kitchen
there is a measure of grace.
Even in the tenements
a babe is born every day
with skin smooth as water,
lungs sucking in life.
I slip a single drop of silver
into each dark, grave eye—
a seed-pearl of hope,
willing this young heart to bloom
with a craving, too.

THE REAL McCOY
(Elijah McCoy invented mechanical self-lubrication.)

Shoveling coal, shoveling coal.
Got to keep the steam up,
got to keep the heat high.
Got to feed this fire in my blood.
I've got skills—"I'M AN ENGINEER!"
I shout above the train's roar,
but I'm still here
stoking up the firebox, shoveling coal.
"I don't care what you did overseas, boy—
in America, a Black Man ain't no engineer."

Mama and Papa rode a train,
a secret railway to freedom.
I've got my own train to ride, I know it!
But steel will seize up if you don't grease it.
And I'll seize up if I don't do something
more than shoveling coal!

Train's stopped, they've got to oil her.
Stupid waste of time—this stop, this job.
This train and I, we both need something.
I need the sweet flow of freedom in my veins.
This train needs a set of veins, too—
to keep her greased, hot and ready to roll.

What if I showed them how to do it,
how to keep their engines running sweet?
What if I thought of a way?
"Stoke 'er up, boy, keep 'er movin'!"
She's moving, all right.
Fire's high, ideas are flying,
greased, hot
and ready to roll.

Humans first flew not in airplanes or gliders but in balloons. In 1783, brothers *Joseph Michel* and *Jacques–Etienne Montgolfier* harnessed the rising capacity of hot air and launched a duck, a sheep, and a rooster above France's royal palace as King Louis XVI watched. The next six years brought a flurry of inventions: Jacques Charles's hydrogen balloon, Sebastien Lenormand's parachute, Jean Baptiste Meusnier's dirigible, and Jean-Pierre Blanchard's airboat. The first human aloft, Francois Pilatre de Rozier, also became the first casualty, when his hydrogen-filled balloon crashed over Boulogne, France.

The first to discover chocolate were Mexico's Aztecs. They ground cacao beans to make a bitter drink (*tchocolatl*) that helped their endurance. Emperor Montezuma II drank up to five gallons a day! Spanish explorer Hernando Cortéz, after brutally conquering the Aztecs, brought cacao beans back to Europe. Sweetened and thinned into "hot chocolate," the drink became wildly popular. *François–Louis Cailler*, a Swiss confectioner, was the first to develop eating chocolate, perfecting a method known as conching—kneading the softened chocolate until smooth and creamy. The cacao plant later earned the botanical name *Theobroma*, or "food of the gods."

Josephine Garis Cochrane grew up in a wealthy home in Chicago. After marrying well, she set up house with the usual army of servants, and soon became famous for elegant dinner parties. Josephine noticed with growing alarm that her expensive imported china was often damaged during washing. Setting up shop in the family woodshed, she designed an automatic dishwasher. Though crude, it did the job so well that friends and even restaurants began inquiring about her machine. She received a patent in 1886 and later founded the company that eventually became Kitchen-Aid.

Against her family's wishes, *Dr. Sara Josephine Baker* studied medicine at home because she couldn't afford to attend college. She obtained her medical degree in 1898, but she didn't gain the respect of her male colleagues until she had worked for years in New York City's worst slums. The high infant mortality rate among the poor appalled her, and in 1910, having been appointed assistant health commissioner of New York, she founded the first government agency devoted to children's health: the Bureau of Public Hygiene. Her simple, preventive measures improved the lives of hundreds of impoverished children.

The son of escaped slaves, *Elijah McCoy* returned to the United States from training in Scotland as a full-fledged railroad engineer. But because he was an African American, he had to settle for a job shoveling coal into a train's firebox. In 1872, during one of many stops to lubricate the train's moving parts, McCoy began thinking of a plan to create canals and chambers within machines to allow for constant lubrication. His method revolutionized not only train travel but industries all over the world. Many copies of his design were made, prompting customers to ask, "Is this the real McCoy?"

A LIGHT
INTERLUDE

DO YA KNOW 'EM?

Do ya know 'em? Can you guess
what they invented? Can you? Yes?
If you can, you'll get a jolt a'
James **Watt** and Alessandro **Volta**
or tap along with Samuel **Morse**
and Wilhelm **Geiger** (Count, of course).
And while you're at it, do not fail
to give a cheer for Louis **Braille**
and his countryman—*le bon docteur*—
the great esteemed Louis **Pasteur**.

To Graf von **Zeppelin**, a large balloon,
with sticking pin, to make it BOOM!
And to Rudolf **Diesel**, clouds of smoke
to make him wheeze and gasp and choke.
Kudos to Amelia **Bloomer**
who must have had a sense of humor,
and to proper old Charles **Macintosh**
who hated rain and snow and frost.
Jules **Leotard**, while very vain,
flexed his muscles to stretch his brain,

(These inventors' names have become synonymous with their inventions.)

while poky old Joseph **Jacquard**
inspected fabric by the yard.
Ever hip is **Levi** Strauss
whose name is known in every house;
but John **McAdam**—would you greet him
if on the pavement you did meet him?
And Alexandre **Eiffel** might,
beside his tower, seem awfully slight.
Let's hear it for Sylvester **Graham**
who tried to make us give up lamb

and more unhealthy stuff, in favor
of crackers that had not much flavor.
To the lusty Earl of **Sandwich**, cheer!
He liked his gambling and his beer
too much to stop! And so instead,
he ate his meals twixt slabs of bread.
And finally let's raise our clapper
to the unforgettable Sir Thomas **Crapper**
who gave us something truly great:
a place to sit and contemplate.

James Watt—This Scottish engineer perfected the steam engine in the late 1700s and invented other devices important to the Industrial Revolution. The "watt," an electrical unit, was named for him.

Alessandro Volta—Volta, an Italian physicist, invented the forerunner of the electrical battery in 1800. The "volt," an electrical unit, was named in his honor.

Samuel Morse—Morse invented the electromagnetic telegraph in 1836, and devised a system of communicating with short and long taps (dots and dashes) known as the Morse code.

Wilhelm Geiger—In 1903, German physicist Hans Wilhelm Geiger created the "Geiger" counter, a device that detects dangerous radioactive substances invisible to the naked eye.

Louis Braille—Blind from age three, this Frenchman became a teacher, musician, and scientist. In 1853 he modified an army coding system to invent "braille," a series of raised dots and dashes that enabled the blind to read by touch.

Louis Pasteur—This influential French chemist founded the science of microbiology by proving that germs cause disease. He developed vaccines and invented "pasteurization," the method of killing bacteria in milk still used today.

Ferdinand Graf von Zeppelin—A German military officer, Zeppelin developed the rigid dirigible in 1900. This cigar-shaped passenger balloon, the "zeppelin," could be steered.

Rudolf Diesel—In 1872 this German engineer invented the internal-combustion engine, and later built the first successful "diesel" engine, utilizing low-cost diesel fuel.

Amelia Bloomer—This self-educated American reformer founded a women's rights newspaper in the 1850s. She appeared at her lectures wearing trousers gathered at the ankle (under a short skirt), which became known as bloomers.

Charles Macintosh—Throughout Great Britain, *mackintosh* is another word for raincoat. Macintosh invented, among other things, the first waterproof fabric in 1823.

Jules Leotard—In 1859 this French trapeze artist pioneered a tight-fitting, stretchy, one-piece garment for his circus acts. "Leotards" are now used in all areas of dance and performance.

Joseph–Marie Jacquard—The son of a French weaver, Jacquard developed a loom that could weave complex patterns mechanically, using a punch-card system. Today, the word *jacquard* refers to a single-color fabric with a raised, intricate weave.

Levi Strauss—Perhaps the single-most important influence on twentieth-century fashion, Strauss invented denim blue jeans (known as Levi's) in 1873. He used innovative rivets at the pocket corners to reinforce points of strain.

John McAdam—This Scottish engineer devised a practical system of road building in 1815. Instead of expensive blocks of stone, he used several layers of crushed, compacted rock, which absorbed the weight of large loads. This type of pavement, still used today, is known as macadam.

Alexandre Gustave Eiffel—To celebrate the centennial of the French Revolution in 1889, this world-renowned French engineer designed and built the Eiffel Tower in Paris. He also helped construct Frederic Auguste Bartholdi's colossal Statue of Liberty in New York.

Sylvester Graham—Possibly the first health-food fanatic, Graham advocated cold showers, hard mattresses, and loose clothing, in addition to the unsifted whole wheat flour that still bears his name. Graham crackers are those made with graham flour.

John Montagu, earl of Sandwich—This English statesman was said to have invented the "sandwich" during an epic, twenty-four-hour gambling stint in 1762, in which he called for bread and meat to keep up his strength.

Thomas Crapper—England led the world in toilets in the 1800s, and Thomas Crapper led England. In 1872 he developed a quiet-flushing toilet utilizing a water cistern, which was known as the crapper.

DAWN
OF THE
MODERN
AGE

THE LIGHT—AH! THE LIGHT
(Marie Curie discovered the principles of radioactivity.)

First of all, I am a Pole.
Manya, they called me
when I was a girl in Warsaw,
under the dark yoke of Russian rule.
We hid our Polish grammars
and spit at the obelisk erected by the Tsar.

But I was drawn to Paris
as a plant is drawn to the light.
And the Sorbonne, despite its
pointed little men,
shone like the sun itself.
Poverty, prejudice, the infuriating
French language—all this,
like a handful of cobwebs,
I swept aside.

For the subject of my doctorate,
I chose uranium.
Just a lump of stone—but it shone!
The work was brutal:
a ton of ore to be hauled, cracked, incinerated
for one pure gram of radium.
I kept a bowl of it at my bedside
so I could wake at night
to its fairy glow.

In the end,
that glow ravaged my skin,
poisoned my blood.
I was like the shell of a burned-out tree.
But what of it?
I, Manya,
the poor Polish girl from Warsaw,
pried open life's hidden heart
and discovered the bright burn
of its decay.

A Length of Pink Ribbon

*(Mary "Caresse" Crosby, daughter of wealthy
socialites, invented the bra in 1913.)*

The problem was air—we hadn't any.
Encased in corsets of whalebone & steel,
how could we breathe?
And, without breath, how could we think?
Run? Laugh? Dance?
It was a cage.
One night, I stepped out.
With a length of pink ribbon
and two handkerchiefs of silk,
I fashioned my own freedom.

What a deep breath I took!
How cool & lovely the silk!
All the long, streaming joy
of my life sprang from that moment.
My head cleared of convention.
Like a newborn infant,
I filled my lungs,
shuddered,
and plunged forth
to feast upon the world.

COCKLEBURS
(In 1948, George de Mestral invented Velcro.)

Piggy-back, irritating burrs
are stuck right to my socks
every day that I hike
among the flowered Alpen rocks!

They grip like mad to the fur
beneath my dear old Fifi's chin
and when I try to rip them off
they catch right onto hair and skin!

Cursed, blasted, sticky-tacky,
aggravating, strong-as-blazes!
What is it that makes you clingy,
Stowaway, that nothing fazes?

Confound it, I'll just pack you off
into my lab to have a look.
Mon Dieu! Beneath a microscope
appears a mass of tiny hooks!

Tiny pincers, little grabbers,
Nature's way of holding fast
till teeth or fingers rip them off
and break their savage grip at last.

Shoelaces will come undone,
buttons pop and zippers split
but these extraordinary hooklets
stay locked tight, a perfect fit.

Tiny hooks . . . little pincers . . .
holding fast to loops of cloth . . .
a new idea beats against my brain
like a persistent moth.

Fifi, *vien*! Let us wander
out among the Alpen rocks
to gather more delightful burrs
that cozy up to fur and socks.

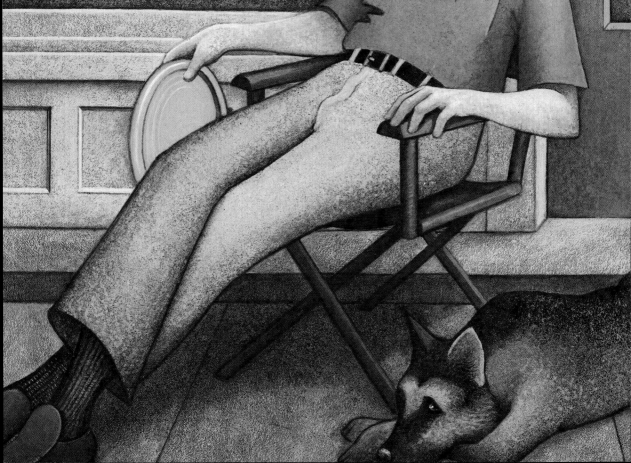

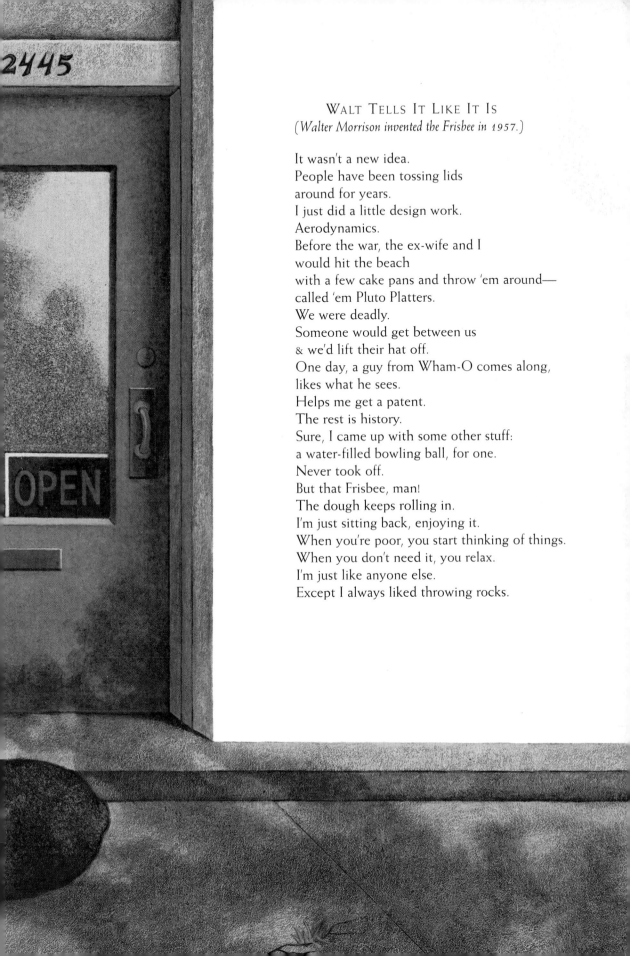

WALT TELLS IT LIKE IT IS
(Walter Morrison invented the Frisbee in 1957.)

It wasn't a new idea.
People have been tossing lids
around for years.
I just did a little design work.
Aerodynamics.
Before the war, the ex-wife and I
would hit the beach
with a few cake pans and throw 'em around—
called 'em Pluto Platters.
We were deadly.
Someone would get between us
& we'd lift their hat off.
One day, a guy from Wham-O comes along,
likes what he sees.
Helps me get a patent.
The rest is history.
Sure, I came up with some other stuff:
a water-filled bowling ball, for one.
Never took off.
But that Frisbee, man!
The dough keeps rolling in.
I'm just sitting back, enjoying it.
When you're poor, you start thinking of things.
When you don't need it, you relax.
I'm just like anyone else.
Except I always liked throwing rocks.

This Is My Life
(Barbara McClintock, Nobel Prize—winning scientist)

This is my life,
if you must know about it,
although I can't see why anyone's interested.
My family didn't have money,
but I managed to reach Cornell.
There, the microscope and I
were introduced to one another.
How can I explain it?
Like going deep into glory;
like sight to a blind man.
Caught in this web of meaning,
I was drawn deeper and deeper.

The outer world intruded.
Upon graduation, I needed a job.
Oh, everyone admired my diligence,
but I was a woman, you see,
fit only for the title of Instructor,
bounced from lab to lab.
I kept working, always working,
spiraling down the long, dizzy chutes
of knowledge.

Then I presented my results.

Now, let's stop here a minute.
Never, never did I want accolades.
Nods of the head from colleagues,
understanding,
a quickening of thought:
those, indeed, I coveted
but failed to gather.
But what does it matter, in the end?
If you know you're right
you don't care what other people think.

It's comical, really,
how we hover and sift and study
when a slim green plant
holds all the secrets.
Sometimes I think I'll sling that Nobel Prize
around a cornstalk.

enquire v.?

(en-kwir): to seek
information by asking
a question

ENQUIRE WITHIN

(Tim Berners-Lee invented the World Wide Web in 1991.)

It began with a brain: mine,
deficient in several respects.
A memory problem—
random connections escape me.
So I built a program linking
all my bits & pieces.
Named it after Mum's musty
old book of Victorian advice:
Enquire Within Upon Everything.

Fast forward ten years:
a computer at every fingertip.
All our bits & pieces—pockets
of knowledge, large and small.
What if they could
all be linked?
Enquire Within Upon Everything.

I flung out the first strands, freely,
and others felt their pull: a revolution
of thousands, worldwide,
all helping weave the Web.

The vision: a system as fast,
as fluid, as flexible as the brain
(not mine).
Anything potentially connected to anything.

The reality? A tool. A marketplace.
A journey toward perfection—
but never, of course, quite there.
Anyone can help:
ask the questions, find the answers,
add a link.
You, perhaps?

Marie Sklodowska Curie was born in Russian-occupied Poland in 1867. After working as a governess, she enrolled at Paris's premier university, the Sorbonne, as the only (much resented) female physics student. Married in 1895 to Pierre Curie, she took up the study of an unknown radiant element in uranium, which she isolated and called radium. Radium, she discovered, had an unstable atomic core, which slowly disintegrated, producing energy. She won the 1903 Nobel Prize in physics with Pierre, and the 1911 Noble Prize in chemistry after his death. She died in 1934 of leukemia, brought on by radiation poisoning. Even today, her notebooks are dangerously radioactive.

In 1913, when *Mary Caresse Crosby* debuted in New York's wealthiest society, women's underclothes were armorlike and extremely uncomfortable. One evening she fashioned her own backless brassiere. So many friends begged her for the design that she filed a patent and eventually started her own lingerie business. She later scandalized New York (and her family) by running off to Paris with poet Harry Crosby to lead a bohemian lifestyle.

The Swiss engineer *George De Mestral* was fond of hiking, and when he returned home, often found burrs firmly attached to his clothing. One day in 1948 he looked at a cocklebur under a microscope and was dumbfounded to discover its secret: hundreds of tiny hooks! Realizing the potential of such a design, he began to experiment. Eight years later he patented a product he called Velcro, from the French words *velours* (velvet) and *croche* (hooked). Velcro is now used not only on clothing but on everything from blood pressure cuffs to antigravity chambers.

Walter Morrison worked as a carpenter for many years before that fateful day in 1957 when he was demonstrating what he called Pluto Platters in a Los Angeles parking lot. A representative of Wham-O Toys in the crowd recognized the potential of Morrison's modified cake pan. Wham-O leased the design and helped Morrison get a patent, changing its name to "Frisbee." Morrison used his Frisbee income to open a hardware store in LaVerne, California, which he claims "doesn't make any money, but it employs a few people and it keeps me off the street."

Barbara McClintock was laughed off the stage when she presented her discoveries about genetics in the 1950s. Her theory about the way genes jump randomly into new positions on chromosomes was simply too extraordinary and complex for most scientists to understand. For forty years she labored alone at Cold Spring Harbor Research Institute studying the inherited traits of corn plants, until the scientific community caught up with her and awarded her the 1983 Nobel Prize in medicine.

The son of two English mathematicians who designed the first commercial computer, *Tim Berners-Lee* (b. 1955) majored in physics at Oxford University. He went on to work at the European Laboratory for Particle Physics (CERN) in Geneva, Switzerland. To aid his own unreliable memory, he developed a software program called Enquire, which allowed him to browse between different research projects using hypertext-highlighted words that jumped to other files. Gradually, he realized that he could expand this system globally through the Internet—a little-used network of linked computers. In 1991, Tim named the universal, decentralized system the World Wide Web, and gave up all patent rights to ensure its unrestricted growth.

809.1
Sid   Sidman, Joyce.
       Eureka! : poems about
       inventors

00201227

ST. LOUIS SCHOOL
LIBRARY
CLARKSVILLE, MD

DEMCO